'I am afraid we must pack our things and set off very soon. The Romans, who rule our country, want everyone to travel to the place where he was born to be registered, counted and taxed. It will be a hard journey for you. Bethlehem is a long way from our town, Nazareth.'

'God will look after us,' Mary reminded her husband.

KT-376-079

The rocky road wound down the hillside.

'We are nearly at Bethlehem now!' Joseph encouraged Mary.

'I am so glad!' she said. 'It's nearly night time. We've slept outside so often, with only the little fire you light to keep wild beasts away. It will be much safer to rest in the yard of an inn with other people. I shall be glad to lie down! My baby will be born soon.'

'Then we must hurry on! Do you see how bare the hills are? King David herded his father's sheep here. Our teachers say that Bethlehem, King David's town, will be the place where the promised king will be born.'

'Hurry, little donkey! God is looking after us. The teachers have told the truth. Our baby king will be born tonight in royal Bethlehem!'

The dinner was cooking: beans and yellow peas bubbled in the pot. Mary was kneading dough. Suddenly a voice called her. She looked up, amazed. A stranger stood beside her. Light shone from his face. 'The Lord is with you, Mary,' he said. 'He is pleased with you. God is giving you a baby boy whose name is to be Jesus. He is the Son of God, the promised king who saves his people.' At first Mary was puzzled. Then she said, 'I am the Lord's servant maid. I will do whatever he says.'

'People said such unkind things when they heard you would have a baby soon,' Joseph the carpenter remembered. 'At first I thought we should not marry.'

'I know. Then God showed you in a dream what to do. You believed him and married me,' Mary smiled.

Their goats played beside them and Mary fondled the wriggling kid. 'Shall we start our journey to Bethlehem before my baby is born?' she asked.

'No room! No room!' the innkeeper cried.

'Please!' Mary begged. 'Everywhere is full. Can't you help?'

'I wish I could, dear! Wait a minute, though. Look . . . this way! You can sleep in the stable. The straw's clean and the cows will keep you warm.' He turned to Joseph. 'Hurry friend. . . You can lay the baby in the manger. It's soft enough, heaped with hay.'

So Jesus was born in a stable, because there was no room anywhere else for him in royal Bethlehem.

'News, good news for everyone!'

The shepherds looked up, terrified. Hundreds of shining messengers, brighter than the starlit sky, crowded round them.

'Don't be afraid,' said one. 'Your promised king, your saviour, has been born. He is close by, in Bethlehem, a baby wrapped in linen cloth, lying in a manger. Go quickly and see.'

'Glory, glory to the most high God! Peace to his people on earth.'

'We came as soon as we heard the news. We left our sheep. The Lord God will guard them from harm.'

Trying to tiptoe, the shepherds crowded into the stable and knelt beside the manger where Jesus slept on the hay.

'Oh, praise God! Thank God! He has sent this little one to be our saviour. The promised king is born in a stable, not in a king's great palace. God has not forgotten us, his poor people.'

Telling everyone the news, the shepherds hurried away, while Mary sat and watched her baby boy.

'It's dark in the stable. The cows low and stamp. Rats run about in the hay, but the music of highest heaven plays for you, dear Jesus. Sleep well, little one. Sleep well,' Mary said.

Wise men came riding towards Bethlehem. Each dry, hot day they rested, shaded by their kneeling camels. At night they rode on, following a bright star. The cold wind stung their faces as they gazed at the sky.

'The star tells me a king is born. I am old, yet when I saw the star I left my home and my books to follow it.'

'It must be guiding us towards the royal palace. Surely we shall find the baby there! The star tells me the newborn child is to be a king of wonder, who will rule for ever.'

The king, Herod, welcomed the wise men, but their news worried him.

'A star tells these visitors that a wonderful king is born in *my* kingdom!' Herod thought. 'Where is this promised king to be born?' he asked the priests.

'In Bethlehem, O king!' The priests bowed, hating their ruler who did not know the promises of God.

'I must get rid of this baby!' Herod decided. '*I* am king in this land.'

'Search for the child in Bethlehem,' Herod told the wise men. 'Tell me where to find him. I wish to bow before him also,' he lied.

The wise men found Mary and Jesus in a house in Bethlehem.

'Here is gold for the King of kings,' said one.

'I have brought sweet-smelling frankincense. I worship God in this small child,' another bowed low.

'Little King, I give you myrrh, for you will heal many hurts, though this will do you harm,' said a third.

'I heard the sound of children crying as we left Bethlehem,' Mary said.

'I heard that sound, too, in my sleep last night. God warned me of terrible danger. Herod plans to kill our baby king,' Joseph said. 'He is sure to send his soldiers after us if he discovers we have gone.'

'Where shall we be safe?' Mary asked.

'God told me to take you and Jesus far away to another country, to Egypt. We shall make our home there until Herod dies. There are many of our own Jewish people in Egypt. We are sure to find friends.'

So the little family lived happily in Egypt until it was safe for them to go home to Nazareth.

'That's fine, Jesus. Pull that end away now!' There were lots of wood shavings on the ground. Jesus liked to play with them.

'Our door is nearly ready!' he shouted to Mary. She smiled at her son. He was growing up so sturdy and strong. No one here in little Nazareth knew about the star, or the wise men with their costly gifts.

When Jesus was twelve years old he travelled to Jerusalem with his parents and other families.

It was wonderful to climb up to the golden Temple! Long after the other families from Nazareth had left, Jesus stayed.

'Who is this boy?' the teachers and priests wondered. 'He knows the writings that tell of God's promises, but even more, he knows God himself in a special way. He is completely at home, here in God's House!'

'Jesus!' Joseph tiptoed in. 'Your mother and I have searched for you for two days!'

'Why have you done this to us?' Mary asked.

'Did you not know I must learn my Father's ways?' Jesus answered and went quietly home with his parents.

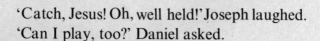

'Catch, Jesus! Oh, well held!' Joseph laughed.

'Can I play, too?' Daniel asked.

'Of course! Join in. We're on our way to Capernaum, the town by the lakeside. I often do repairs for the fishermen, and Jesus likes to help.'

'I like to see my cousins, too,' Jesus said. 'Ready, Daniel? Catch!'

Mary sat in the shade. Sometimes she wondered if it had all been a dream: the splendid messenger who told her the news about her child; the excited shepherds who praised God for sending the promised king; the wise men who bowed before her baby; the escape into Egypt. They were such an ordinary family! Yet in her heart she knew that, one day, Jesus would leave her. He would put away his carpenter's tools and do the work God his Father planned: bringing the love of God to everyone.

Glory to God!

The angel told Mary that her baby, Jesus, would be the promised king.

Hundreds of years before Jesus was born God told the Jews that he would send someone special to be their king. The Jewish prophets told the people about the day when he would come. They even said that he would be born in Bethlehem. That is why the priests were able to tell Herod where the baby king was to be found.

Look back through the book and see how many times the word 'promise' or 'promised' comes in the story.

When the shepherds and the wise men knew that Jesus had been born they wanted to show how glad they were. The shepherds sang praises to God as they went back to their sheep. They were probably the very first men to sing a Christmas carol! Since then all sorts of people have written carols and hymns to show their joy at the birth of Jesus. Can you think of any that we still sing at Christmas?

The wise men showed how glad they were by bringing presents for the baby. We give presents to one another at Christmas. What are some of the other ways that you and your family show your happiness at this time?